One Hundred Graces

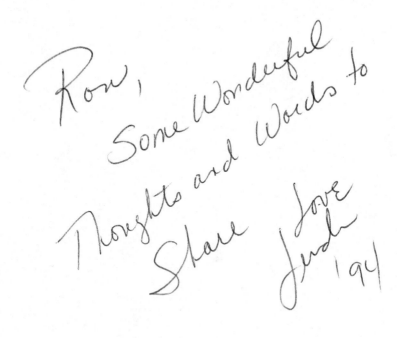

Ron,

Some Wonderful
Thoughts and Words to
Share

Love
Linda
'94

One Hundred GRACES

Selected by Marcia and Jack Kelly

◆

with calligraphy by Christopher Gausby

Bell Tower / New York

A percentage of the royalties from this book will go to the Seva Foundation to help fund its worldwide program of compassionate action ⟶

Grateful acknowledgment is made for permission to reprint the graces on the following pages: 12, © 1992 by Robert Lax; 15, from Kripalu Kitchen, © Kripalu Yoga Fellowship 1980; 18, from Complete Sayings of Hazrat Inayat Khan, Omega Publications Inc., New Lebanon, NY; 22, 35, & 46, © 1992 by Father John Giuliani; 24-6, from To Be a Jew: A Guide to Jewish Observance in Contemporary Life by Rabbi Hayim Halevy Donin. copyright © 1972 by the author. Reprinted by permission of Basic Books, a division of HarperCollins Publishers Inc.; 37-9, from Present Moment, Wonderful Moment by Thich Nhat Hanh, Parallax Press; 30, 70, & 77, from Prayers for the Domestic Church by Edward Hays, 1980, Forest of Peace Books Inc., Easton, Kansas; 48 & 74 from The Tassajara Recipe Book by Edward Espe Brown, Shambhala Publications; 52 & 61, copyright © 1991 by Evelyn Avoglia; 54, from The Blessing Cup by Rock Travnikar, O.F.M., St. Anthony Messenger Press; 67, from Table Prayer by M. D. Bouyer, The Crossroad Publishing Co., New York; 106, from The Dhammapada, copyright © 1976 by Thomas Byrom, Alfred A. Knopf, Inc.; 110, from Openings, copyright © 1968 by Wendell Berry. Reprinted by permission of Harcourt Brace Jovanovich, Inc. ⟶

Copyright © 1992 by Marcia Kelly and Jack Kelly

Foreword copyright © 1992 by Toinette Lippe

Published by Bell Tower, an imprint of Harmony Books, a division of Crown Publishers, Inc., 201 East 50th Street, New York, New York 10022. Member of the Crown Publishing Group.

Harmony, Bell Tower, and colophon are registered trademarks of Crown Publishers, Inc.

Manufactured in the United States of America

Library of Congress Cataloging-in-Publication Data

One hundred graces / selected by Marcia and Jack Kelly; with
  calligraphy by Christopher Gausby. — 1st ed.
      p.   cm.
    1. Grace at meals. I. Kelly, Marcia. II. Kelly, Jack, 1934–
  III. Gausby, Christopher. IV. Title: 100 graces.
  BV283.G7054 1992
  242'.2 — dc20
                                                      91-40464
                                                      CIP

ISBN 0-517-58567-7   10 9 8 7 6 5 4 3

❖ Contents ❖

❖ Foreword ❖

by Toinette Lippe

Saying grace is an ancient and vital tradition the world over. To begin with, it provides a **space**, a moment of **stillness**, in which to relinquish the activities of the day and allow the mind to settle ❖ Then, as we acknowledge the source of our nourishment, we are filled with astonishment at the generosity of the Creator, with **gratitude**, and with praise. In bringing the body, mind, and heart together, we come to ourselves, and remember who we are and why we are here. For some families a meal is the only time everyone is present and so the opportunity to enjoy one another and really celebrate the occasion is not to be lost. For many, a meal is also the only time that there is any **memory** of the **Divine.** Saying grace establishes an immediate connection with that memory. In such a moment, when our minds are clear and the truth is reinforced by being sounded aloud, we can dedicate the meal and the strength we receive from it to the **service** of whoever or whatever is before us ❖

G·r·a·c·e

By Robert Lax ❖

grace
be
fore
breath
ing
❖
grace
while
breath
ing
❖
grace
af
ter
breath
ing
❖
be
fore
eat
ing
❖
af
ter
eat
ing
❖
while
eat
ing

grace
be
fore
each
good
&
need
ed
❖
ac
tion
❖
each
ac
tiv
i
ty
❖
grace
at
eve
ry
❖
mo
ment
❖
of
our
lives
❖
grace
be
fore
dy
ing

grace
be
fore
birth
❖
thanks
&
bless
ing
❖
to
ac
com
pan
y
❖
eve
ry
mo
ment
❖
of
our
lives
❖
grace
ful
grace
❖
grace
grace-
giving

calls
forth
bless
ing
❖

&
gives
thanks
❖

for
bless
ings
❖

grace
is
thanks
❖

our
thanks
❖

for
every
❖

bless
ing
❖

grace
be
fore
❖

dream
ing
❖

grace
be
fore
sleep
❖

grace
while
dream
ing

grace
in
sleep
❖

grace
af
ter
dream
ing
❖

grace
af
ter
sleep
❖

grace
for
the
bless
ing
❖

of
dreams
&
sleep
❖

grace
is
bless
ing
❖

a
thanks
for
bless
ing
❖

a
thanks
for
be
ing
a
ble

to
thank
❖

for
bless
ings
❖

for
be
ing
❖

so
blessed
❖

for
be
ing
❖

so
graced
❖

as
to
be
❖

ev
er
❖

a
ble
❖

to
thank
❖

for
grace

❖

❖

❖

❖

❖

❖ Affirmation to My Body ❖

I recognize you are the temple in which
my spirit and creative energy dwell.

I have created you from my need to have my
spirit manifest on earth so that I may have
this time to learn and grow.

I offer you this food so that you may
continue to sustain my creative energy,
my spirit, my soul.

I offer this food to you with love, and a
sincere desire for you to remain free from
disease and disharmony.

I accept you as my own creation.

I need you.
I love you.

❖ From Kripalu Kitchen

15

Be present at our table, Lord ❖
Be here and everywhere adored ❖
Thy creatures bless and grant that we
May feast in Paradise with Thee ❖

John Cennick (1718 ❖ 1755)

On the Upper West Side of New York City there is
a wonderful group called Project Reachout
(a project of Goddard-Riverside Community
Center), who work with the homeless people
who are mentally ill. At their special program,
"The Other Place," a theatrical session was
held and the topic was mealtime graces.
Nineteen of the members present that day had
a grace to contribute. This was one of them.

George ❖ Gary ❖ Dusty ❖ Anton ❖ Leo ❖ Joe
Barbara ❖ Billy ❖ Phil ❖ Florence ❖ Frank
Bradley ❖ Laverne ❖ Carl ❖ Maria ❖ Marshall
Manuel ❖ Gregory ❖ Philip ❖ John ❖ Diane
Ed ❖ Nelida

Be the eye of God betwixt me and each eye ✢

the purpose of God betwixt me and each purpose ✢

the hand of God betwixt me and each hand ✢

the shield of God betwixt me and each shield ✢

the desire of God betwixt me and each desire ✢

the bridle of God betwixt me and each bridle ✢

And no mouth can curse me ✢ ∿∿∿∿

The pain of Christ betwixt me and each pain ✢

the love of Christ betwixt me and each love ✢

the dearness of Christ betwixt me and each dearness ✢

the kindness of Christ betwixt me and each kindness ✢

the wish of Christ betwixt me and each wish ✢

the will of Christ betwixt me and each will ✢

And no venom can wound me ✢ ∿∿∿∿

For centuries it was the custom in Scotland
to say a blessing before any action. This is
one of the Gaelic graces collected by
Alexander Carmichael in the nineteenth
century and used in Avery Brooke's
∿∿∿∿ CELTIC PRAYERS ∿∿∿

Beloved Lord ❖
    almighty God ❖
through the
    rays of the sun ❖
through the
    waves of the air ❖
through the
    all-pervading
    life in space ❖
purify and revivify me,
and I pray,
    heal my body, heart,
    and soul ❖
Amen ❖

Nayaz
by Hazrat Inayat Khan

eloved Lord,
we do greatly thank You
for the abundance
that is ours ❖

ß·I·S·M·I·L·L·A·h

al-Rahman al-Rahim

(In the name of the compassionate and beneficent God)

This Islamic invocation is
used *before any action,* but
particularly before meals.
It is said that Muhammad
(peace be upon him) recited
a longer form of this blessing:

"O Lord, bless this food and
protect us from the doom
of fire ❖ In the name of God
we begin our meal."

Translation by
Dr. Adil H. Al-Humadi

BLESS, O LORD,

this food to our use
And us to Thy loving

service

Bless our hearts

❖ to hear in the

❖ breaking of bread the

❖ Song of the Universe ❖

Father John Giuliani ✦
The Benedictine Grange ✦
West Redding, Connecticut ✦

22

Blessed are you,
O Lord our God,
Eternal King,

Who feeds the whole world
With Your goodness,
With grace, with loving kindness,
And with tender mercy.

You give food to all flesh,
For Your loving kindness endures forever.
Through Your great goodness,
Food has never failed us.
O may it not fail us forever,
For Your name's sake, since You
Nourish and sustain all living things
And do good to all,
And provide food for all Your creatures
Whom You have created.

Blessed are You, O Lord,
who gives food to all.

Hebrew *berakhah* (blessing)

Blessed art Thou, O Lord our God, King of the universe, through whose word all things were called into being ❖

From
To Be a Jew: A Guide to
Jewish Observance in
Contemporary Life
by
Rabbi Hayim Halevy Donin

Blessed Art Thou, O Lord our God,

King of the universe, who creates many living beings and the things they need ❖ For all that thou hast created to sustain the life of every living being, blessed be thou, the— Life of the universe.

From To Be a Jew by Rabbi Hayim Halevy Donin

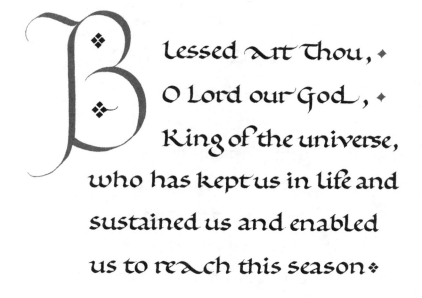

Blessed art Thou, ◆
O Lord our God, ◆
King of the universe,
who has kept us in life and
sustained us and enabled
us to reach this season ❖

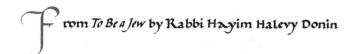

From *To Be a Jew* by Rabbi Hayim Halevy Donin

Come, let us welcome the Sabbath.

May its radiance illumine our hearts

as we kindle these tapers ❖ ❖ ❖

May the Lord bless us with Sabbath joy.

May the Lord bless us with Sabbath holiness.

May the Lord bless us with Sabbath peace.

This grace is said in a traditional Jewish
home before the meal on Friday evening,
as the candles are lit to welcome the Sabbath.

Come, Lord Jesus!

I open my mind and heart and soul,
And long for You to be born anew in me.
Help me to experience Your presence within me,
And to allow You to touch the earth through me.

Come, Lord Jesus!

Come and stay with my family and friends—
And all who are dear to me. Be near
Especially those who are burdened by
Sickness or sadness— set them free
By Your love and care.

Come, Lord Jesus!

Bring peace to our world. May we hear again
Your own prayer: "That we may be one."
And may we learn anew to follow Your example:
"That there may be bread" for all.

We hunger, we thirst, we wait for You!
Come, Lord Jesus!
And do not delay!

This Advent prayer comes
from Sallie Latkovich, CSJ, of
the Mother of God House of Prayer
in Alva, Florida

Creator, Earth Mother, we thank You for our lives and this beautiful day ❖ Thank You for the bright SUN and the rain we received last night ❖ Thank You for this circle of friends and the opportunity to be together ❖ ❖ We want to thank You especially at this time for the giveaway of their lives made by the chickens, beets, carrots, grains, and lettuce ❖ ❖ We thank them for giving of their lives so we may continue our lives through this great blessing ❖ Please help us honor them through how we live our lives ❖ ❖

Mary Fallahay of the Bear Tribe Medicine Society, Spokane, Washington. This grace was created in honor of the meal we had together on May 2, 1991 ❖

The day is coming to a close,

   and, like the disciples on the road to Emmaus,

   we pause to break bread together.

May our eyes be opened,

   and, in this act of common sharing,

   may we see the Risen Lord in one another.

May we see the Lord of Life in our food,

   our conversation, and lives shared in common.

May the blessing of God,

   His peace and love,

   rest upon our table.

Alleluia! Amen.

Evening meal blessing for Easter by Edward Hays
   of Shantivanam, Easton, Kansas

Dearest Lord, teach me to be generous.

Teach me to serve Thee as Thou deservest;

To give and not to count the cost;

To fight and not to heed the wounds;

To toil and not to seek reward,

Save that of knowing that

I do Thy will, o God.

St. Ignatius Loyola
(1491 — 1556)

Deep peace of the shining star *to you*,
Deep peace of *the running wave* to you,
Deep peace of the quiet earth *to you*,
Deep joy of *the leaping fire* to you,
Deep peace of the Son of Peace *to you*.

ELTIC prayer from *Sister Susan,*
Nada Hermitage, Crestone, Colorado

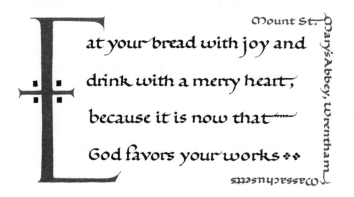

Eat your bread with joy and drink with a merry heart, because it is now that God favors your works ✦✦

Mount St. Mary's Abbey, Wrentham, Massachusetts

The eyes of all wait upon Thee
And Thou givest them their meat in due season.

❖ Thou openest Thy hand ❖

And fillest all things living with plenteousness.

We thank Thee, O Lord, for these

Thy gifts and beseech Thee to grant

that whether we eat or drink

or whatsoever we do, ❖ ❖ ❖ ❖

—all may be done to Thy glory.

At some monasteries the first four
lines—which are from Psalm 104,
verses 27 and 28—are read
responsively ❖

Faithful God,

let this table be a sign of tomorrow's hope already here, when with the world which hungers for your justice and peace, we shall come together singing your name as our very own ❖ ❖

Father ❖ ❖ ❖ John Giuliani, The Benedictine Grange, ❖ ❖ ❖ West Redding, Connecticut

Father,

bless this food which ～～

re-creates our bodies ❖

May the hearing of Your word

re-create our souls ❖❖

Mount St. Mary's Abbey,
Wrentham, Massachusetts

Five Gathas by the Vietnamese Buddhist monk

Thich Nhat Hanh

Serving Food

In this food
I see clearly
the presence *of* the entire universe
supporting my existence.

❖

Looking at the Plate filled with food

All living beings
are struggling for life.
May they all have
enough food to eat today.

Just Before Eating

The plate is filled with food.
I am aware that each morsel is
the fruit of much hard work
by those who produced it.

Beginning to Eat

With the first taste,

I promise to practice loving kindness.

With the second,

I promise to relieve the suffering of others.

With the third,

I promise to see others' joy as my own.

With the fourth,

I promise to learn the way of
            nonattachment and equanimity.

This verse is said while taking the first
four mouthfuls of food. They are a
reminder of the Four Immeasurable
States: loving kindness, compassion,
sympathetic joy, and nonattachment.

Finishing the Meal

The plate is empty.

My hunger is satisfied.

I vow to live

for the benefit of all beings.

Food —

God's love
made edible ❖
May we be
swept into
your presence ❖

Brother Thomas,
Nada Hermitage ❖
Crestone, Colorado

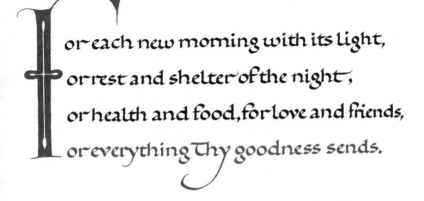

For each new morning with its light,
or rest and shelter of the night,
or health and food, for love and friends,
or everything Thy goodness sends.

Ralph Waldo Emerson {1803 — 1882}

Give food to the hungry,
O Lord, and
hunger for you
to those who
have food ❖

Give us
This day

our daily bread, O Father
in heaven, and grant that we
who are filled with good things
from Your open hand may never
close our hearts to the hungry,
the homeless, and the poor;
in the name of the Father,
and of the Son, and of
the Holy Spirit ❖

Abbey of New Clairvaux,
Vina, California

Give us this day
our daily bread,
O Father in heaven,
and grant that we
who gather here in
fellowship of faith
and love, may take
our food with
gladness and
simplicity of
heart ❖ ❖ ❖ ❖

Abbey of New Clairvaux,
Vina, California ❖ ❖

God, I thank you for the blessings and gifts that You have provided for me and my relatives, and the *food* that You have provided also. I pray that we will receive *strength* and *good health* from it ❖ So be it ❖

Lakota grace translated by *Bill Quejas*

God of pilgrims,
give us always a table to stop at
where we can tell our
story and sing
our song ✦ ✦ ✦ ✦

Father John Giuliani,
The Benedictine Grange,
West Redding, Connecticut

GOD to enfold me, GOD to surround me,

GOD in my speaking, GOD in my thinking.

GOD in my sleeping, GOD in my waking,

GOD in my watching, GOD in my hoping.

GOD in my life, GOD in my lips,

GOD in my soul, GOD in my heart.

GOD in my sufficing, GOD in my slumber,

GOD in mine ever-living soul, GOD in mine serenity.

This Gaelic grace was collected
by Alexander Carmichael
in the nineteenth century
and used in Avery Brooke's
CELTIC PRAYERS ❖

47

I do this chore
not just to get it
out of the way
but as the way
to make real
kind connected mind.

May I awaken to what
these ingredients offer,
and may I awaken best I can
energy, warmth, imagination,
this offering of heart and hand.

From The Tassajara Recipe Book
by Edward Espe Brown

I offer You this day
All I shall think, do, say for:
(peace in the world)

(Everyone at the table then states
his or her own intention for the day.)

Don George,
La Casa de Maria,
Santa Barbara, California

I slept and dreamt
⁜ that life was joy,
I awoke and saw that
⁜ life was service.
I acted and B·E·H·O·L·D,
⁜ service was joy.

RABINDRANATH TAGORE
(1861–1941)

I was regretting the past
and fearing the future.
Suddenly God was speaking.
"My name is 'I Am.'" I waited.
God continued,

"When you live in the past,
with its mistakes and regrets,
it is hard. I am not there.
My name is not 'I was.'

When you live in the future,
with its problems and fears, it is hard.
I am not there.
My name is not 'I will be.'

When you live in this moment,
it is not hard. I am here.
My name is 'I Am.'"

from Helen Mellicost (on the kitchen wall of the
Ranch Guesthouse ❖ St. Benedict's Monastery ❖
Snowmass, Colorado)

I will sing to You, O sing to You.
You have been good to me.

Air and fire, earth and water
Reveal Your face to me.
O Maker of the universes,
you have been good to me ◆

War and famine, peace and plenty
Reveal Your face to me.
God of time and endless ages,
You have been good to me ◆

Song and story, word and wonder
Reveal Your face to me.
Holy Wisdom of all nations,
you have been good to me ◆

Hands and labor, hearts and longing
Reveal Your face to me.
Loving Maker of the people,
you have been good to me ◆

Evelyn Avoglia of Bridgeport,
Connecticut, wrote this
"Song of the Four Scriptures"
based on a lecture by
Father Thomas Berry.

In India, when we meet and part we often say "Namaste,"[#] which means I honor the place in you where the entire universe resides, I honor the place in you of love, of light, of truth, of peace. I honor the place within you ❖ ❖ ❖ ❖ ❖ ❖

Where if you are in that place in you
And I am in that place in me,

There is only $\left(\begin{smallmatrix} n \\ e \end{smallmatrix}\right)$ of us ❖

From *Grist for the Mill*
by Ram Dass

[#] pronounced *namastay*

In the spirit of humble prayer we give thanks.

For our family, friends, relatives,
and those who teach us of God's way,
❖we pray❖
We thank You, Lord.
For our home and for the many things
You surround us with in goodness,
❖we pray❖
For all creation‿,
for sights and sounds and all our senses,
❖we pray❖

(Anyone at the table may add a
petition or request after this.)

From *The Blessing Cup* by Rock Travnikar, OFM

54

❖ Joining Hands ❖

Everyone at the table

joins hands for a

silent moment ❖

Quaker grace

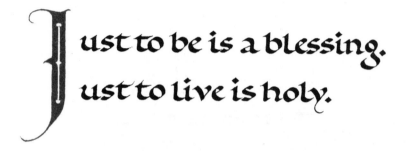

Just to be is a blessing.
Just to live is holy.

Abraham Joshua Heschel

K NOW, TOO, FROM ME

Shineth the gathered glory of the suns

Which lighten all the world: from Me the moons

Draw silvery beams, and fire fierce loveliness.

I penetrate the clay, and lend all shapes

Their living force; I glide into the plant —

Root, leaf, and bloom - to make the woodlands green

With springing sap. Becoming vital warmth,

I glow in glad, respiring frames, and pass,

With outward and with inward breath, to feed

The body by all meats.

The Song Celestial or
Bhagavad Gita ❖
Translated from the
Sanskrit by Sir Edwin Arnold

Let there be peace on earth
and let it begin with me ❖
Let there be peace on earth
and let it begin with me ❖
Let there be peace on earth
and let it begin with me ❖

Peace in our food,
Peace in our bodies,
Peace in our home,
Peace in our world,
Thanks, God ❖ Amen ❖

The Rev. Dr. Barbara King,
Hillside International Truth Center,
Atlanta, Georgia

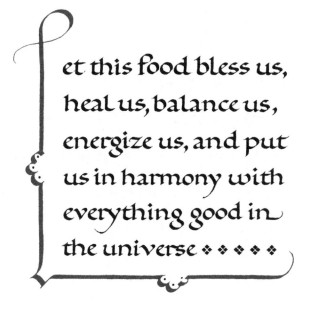

et this food bless us,
heal us, balance us,
energize us, and put
us in harmony with
everything good in
the universe ❖ ❖ ❖ ❖ ❖

Theo Levine and Sonya Heller

Let us give thanks for this food
And Thy blessing and benediction be upon it.
May our hands so energize this food
That it supplies the needs of our bodies
And may we be moved to share with others
What they are in need of ❖ ❖ ❖ ❖ ❖

This blessing, from the Sakya Monastery in Seattle, Washington, is said with everyone raising their hands (palms down) over the food ❖ ❖ ❖ ❖

Listen, my soul. This is your task :
To bless the holy name of Yahweh and
remember all God's kindnesses ❖
Remember your offenses and know
    they are forgiven ❖
Remember your diseases and know
    that they are healed ❖
Remember your death and know
    that you are living ❖
Know that this tender love is
    Yahweh's way with you ❖
A fool may ask for justice, but
    Yahweh gives us mercy ❖
Our sins deserve God's anger, but
    we are given love ❖
All within me sings :
    Yahweh is our loving God
Whose mercy is upon us ; bless your God, my soul ❖

Evelyn Avoglia of Bridgeport, Connecticut,
was inspired to write this through
reading the Psalms

61

LORD, bless our ears with Your word.

Bless our bodies with Your bounties. ❖ ❖ ❖

Bless our lives with Your love. ❖ ❖ ❖ ❖ ❖ ❖

Mount St. Mary's Abbey,
Wrentham, Massachusetts ❖

Lord,

bless our meal,

and as you satisfy

the needs of

each of us,

make us mindful

of the needs

of others ❖

❖ Mount St. Mary's Abbey, Wrentham, Massachusetts ❖

Lord,

bless our shared meal,

a sacrament to

our shared

unity.

Mount St. Mary's Abbey,
Wrentham, Massachusetts

The Lord bless you and keep you :

The Lord make His face to shine upon you,

and be gracious unto you :

The Lord lift up His countenance upon you,

and give you peace.

Numbers 6:24-26

This was the blessing bestowed upon the people in
the ancient temple by the high priest, as
commanded in the Torah. Today it is
incorporated into the service by the
rabbi or by descendants of the ancient
holy families. If the person giving this
blessing is very observant and pious, it
is accompanied by a special hymn and
sung with the face covered by a *tallit*
(prayer shawl). A favorite childhood
Sunday school teacher, Joseph M. Bear,
explained this to us recently. Little did
he expect to be our teacher well into
adulthood

**ORD** make me an instrument of your peace.
Where there is hatred, let me sow love;
where there is injury, pardon;
, where there is doubt, faith;
where there is darkness, light;
and where there is sadness, joy.
O Divine Master, grant that I may not
so much seek to be consoled as to console;
to be understood as to understand;
to be loved as to love,

For it is in giving that we receive,
it is in pardoning that we are pardoned,
and it is in dying that we are born to

eternal life.

St. Francis of Assisi
(1182?-1226)

Lord our God,

You invite us
to the banquet of your wisdom,
giving us for nourishment
both the bread of the earth
and your living word ❖
Bless this meal,
and grant us entry to your banquet ❖
In the name of the Father,
and of the Son,
and of the holy Spirit ❖ Amen ❖

from Table Prayer by M. D. Bouyer

LORD,

we begin this meal
by giving thanks to You.

This food is the
gift of Your creation.
Protect that creation
from all harm and hatred.

May we cherish the earth
and all who partake of its
richness.

May we choose life and peace
so that we and all your
children may live.

We offer our thanks to You.
Our God of peace, through Jesus,
the Prince of Peace. Amen

SCJ Office of Justice and Peace
Priests of the Sacred Heart
Hales Corners, Wisconsin

Lord,

we have been nourished
by our meal and by
Your presence with us ❖

Give us the strength
to build a unity of love
among ourselves and
friends and others ❖

Help us to grow in Your ways
which are the ways of peace ❖

We offer this prayer
through Jesus who is
our Way, our Truth,
and our Life ❖ Amen

SCJ Office of Justice and Peace
Priests of the Sacred Heart
Hales Corners, Wisconsin

LORD, You who gave bread
to Moses and his people
    while they traveled in the desert,
    come now, and bless these
    gifts of food
    which You have given to us ❖
As this food gives up its life for us,
    may we follow that pattern of
    self-surrender for each other
May we BE life to one another.

From
Prayers for the
Domestic Church
by Edward Hays

M ay all beings have happiness
   and the causes of happiness ❖

M ay all beings be free from sorrow
   and the causes of sorrow ❖

M ay all never be separated from
   the sacred happiness which is sorrowless ❖

M ay all live in equanimity,
   without attachment or aversion,
   believing in the equality of all that lives ❖

N yingma Institute,
   Berkeley, California

May God bless

our meal and grant us a
compassionate and
understanding heart
toward one another ❖

Mount St. Mary's Abbey,
Wrentham, Massachusetts

May He who comes
bless our meal and
enable us to discern
His coming in every
grace-filled moment
of our lives ❖ ❖ ❖ ❖ ❖

Mount St. Mary's Abbey
Wrentham, Massachusetts

May I,
together with all beings,
enjoy the pure taste
of kind mind joyful mind big mind ❖

From *Tassajara Recipe Book*
by Edward Espe Brown

May light and love surround us and *guide us to right action* ❖

A blessing given to our friend,
Linda Moscarella, at a meeting
at the Universalist Church,
New York City

May love,
joy, and
peace be
yours in
abundance ❖

Larry and Girija Brilliant

May our home be made holy, O God, by Your light.

May the light of love and truth shine upon us all

as a blessing from You ❖ ❖ ❖

May our table and our family

be consecrated by Your Divine Presence

at this meal and at all our family meals. Amen.

From *Prayers for the Domestic Church*
by Edward Hays

This blessing is recited as
the candles are lit for
the Jewish sabbath ❖

May prayerful peace flow outward from here,

Touching with grace all those

Whom you love and all the earth as well. Amen.

Our Lady of Solitude House of Prayer,
Black Canyon City, Arizona

May the blessing of God rest upon you,
May his peace abide with you, ❖ ❖ ❖
May his presence illuminate your heart
Now and forevermore. ❖ ❖ ❖ ❖ ❖ ❖ ❖ ❖

Sufi blessing

❖ OM ❖

~May the Gods through our senses enjoy this food ❖

May we always be just a witness
and let the food nourish and strengthen
     our bodies and minds
so that we can climb up to the last step of Yoga.
(Bliss, self-realization, God-realization,
                  samadhi)

OM shanti, shanti, shanti ❖

OM is a sacred syllable which both embraces all things and is the cause of their creation. It is often sounded at the commencement and conclusion of a prayer. The lips are rounded and the sound "O" rises steadily from deep in the body. The lips gradually close in a strong humming which resonates in the nose. The Sanskrit word shanti is pronounced with a long "ā", as in "ah", and a very short lilting "i." Repeated thrice in this way, it can be understood to mean "May peace and peace and peace be everywhere." Generally all present join in sounding OM even if the rest of the grace is spoken by one person.

This mealtime blessing is used by Dharma Mittra at special celebrations with his yoga students in New York.

May the Lord

accept this, our offering,
and bless our food that
it may bring us strength
in our body, vigor in our
mind, and selfless
devotion in our
heart for his
service ✣

Swami Paramananda,
Book of Daily Thoughts and Prayer

May the words of our
mouths *and the* meditations
of our hearts be acceptable
in Thy sight, O Lord.

Psalm 19:14

May there always be work for your hands to do

May your purse always hold a coin or two

May the sun always shine upon your window pane

May a rainbow be certain to follow each rain

May the hand of a friend always be near to you &

May God fill your heart with gladness to cheer you.

An Irish blessing

May we be
a channel of blessings
for all that we meet ❖

Edgar Cayce

Now that I am about to eat, O great Spirit, give my thanks to the beasts and birds whom You have provided for my hunger, and pray deliver my sorrow that living things must make a sacrifice for my comfort and well-being. Let the feather of corn spring up in its time and let it not wither but make full grains for the fires of our cooking pots, now that I am about to eat.

A Native American grace
from The Lama Foundation,
San Cristobal, New Mexico

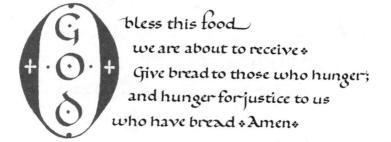

GOD bless this food
we are about to receive ✦
Give bread to those who hunger;
and hunger for justice to us
who have bread ✦ Amen ✦

This grace is used in many places
around the world. One source
said that it came from Nicaragua
and another that it was part of
the liturgy of the French
Community of the Ark,
a working order of men and
women who put into daily
practice Gandhi's principles of
nonviolence and dedication to
truth ✦

O GOD, you are the giver of every good and perfect gift ❖ ❖ we are aware of how easily we take and how often we grudgingly give ❖ Give us the gift of grateful hearts, that we may want to share freely with others all you have given us ❖ Amen ❖

St. Paul the Apostle Monastery,
Palm Desert, California ❖ ❖ ❖

O gracious God,
when You open Your hand,
You satisfy the desires of every living thing.
Bless the land and waters;
give the world a plentiful harvest;
let your spirit go forth
to renew the face of the earth.
As You show Your love and kindness
in the bounty of the land and sea,
save us from selfish use of Your gifts,
so that women and men everywhere
may give You thanks, for Jesus' sake. Amen.

Holden Village,
Chelan, Washington

O Lord God,

who has called us Your servants
to ventures of which we cannot
see the ending, by paths as yet
untrodden and through perils
unknown:

Give us Faith

to go out with good courage,
not knowing where we go, but
only that Your hand is leading
us and Your love supporting us.
Amen ❖

Holden Village,
Chelan, Washington

O Thou who clothes the lilies,

Who feeds the birds of the sky,

Who leads the lambs to pasture,

And the deer to the waterside,

Who multiplied loaves and fishes,

And changed the water to wine,

Do Thou come to our table as giver

And as our guest to dine.

Once they saw a star
that pointed to a promised land,
to a land of peace.
Peacemakers set out to follow that star.

It is both a joyful and arduous journey.
Sometimes the star shines brightly,
the promise seems certain,
and the pilgrims can sing,
"How beautiful are the feet of those
who bring God's peace."
Often the star disappears,
clouded over, hidden from view,
and the pilgrims grope blindly,
grow discouraged, get weary,
give thought to settling down,
to forgetting the promise of peace.

One thing is certain:
all pilgrims need nourishment
to sustain the journey.
An occasional oasis for the spirit
is essential,
a time to feast on the refreshing waters,
the rich food of the spirit
in order to get strength
to continue the pilgrimage through darkness,
star-shine or not.

Mary Lou Kownacki, OSB, of the Catholic peace movement.
Pax Christi USA, Erie, Pennsylvania

Our Father,

we are grateful for this
family, who hand in hand

form 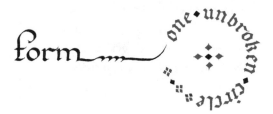 one · unbroken · circle · · ·

Help us to do Thy will,

as caring individuals
and as a loving
family ✦ Amen ✦

PRAISE, praise to the father
praise, praise·to·the· son
praise, praise·to·the· spirit
All · praise·to·the · three
in One.

BLESS each of our families
less this food we eat
May we be a blessing
To all that we meet ❖
Amen ❖

Christian Renewal Center,
Silverton, Oregon

Praise to the Lord

of all creation,

Glory to God,

the fount of grace;

May peace abide

in every nation,

Goodwill to all

of every race ❖❖

Raising Our Plates

All who are at
the table raise
their plates for
a quiet moment.

Recall the face of the poorest and most helpless man whom you may have seen and ask yourself if the step you contemplate is going to be of any use to him. Will it restore him to a control over his own life and destiny? Will it lead to self-rule for the hungry and spiritually starved millions of our fellow men? ❖ ❖ ❖

If so, then you will find your doubts and yourself melting away.

The Gandhi Talisman

The seed of God is in us ❖
Given an intelligent and
hardworking farmer, it will
thrive and grow up into God,
whose seed it is; and accordingly
its fruits will be God-nature ❖
Pear seeds grow into pear trees,
nut seeds into nut trees, and
❖ God seeds into God ❖

Meister Eckhart
(1260–1329)

SING TO GOD,

Sing praises to His name.
Lift up a song to Him
Who rides upon the clouds;
His name is the Lord.
Exalt before Him.

Psalm 68:4

The Selkirk Grace

Some hae meat, and canna eat,
And some wad eat that want it,
But we hae meat and we can eat,
And sae the lord be thankit ❖ ❖

Robert Burns

Thank heaven for this food and for this company. May it be good for us ❖

Damianos Theodosios, Patmos, Greece

Thanks to Thee, O God, that I have risen today,
To the rising of this life itself;
May it be to Thine own glory,
O God of every gift,
And to the glory of my soul likewise.
O great God, aid Thou my soul
With the aiding of Thine own mercy;
Even as I clothe my body with wool,
Cover Thou my soul with the shadow of Thy wing.
Help me to avoid every sin,
and the source of every sin to forsake;
And as the mist scatters on the crest of the hills,
May each ill haze clear from my soul, O God.

This Gaelic grace was collected by
Alexander Carmichael in the
nineteenth century and used in
Avery Brooke's *Celtic Prayers*.

There is only one caste,
　　　　the caste of humanity;
There is only one religion,
　　　　the religion of love;
There is only one language,
　　　　the language of the heart.

Sathya Sai Baba

This is a time for GIVING THANKS
This is a time for remembrance ❖

Let us remember all those
who are united with us and
GIVE THANKS for that bond of union…

Let us remember our past and
GIVE THANKS for what we have become…

Let us be present in the present and
GIVE THANKS for the here-and-now…

Let us re-member our future and
GIVE THANKS for all that is to happen to us…

Let us GIVE THANKS for the whole universe
especially for our creation
        and the life that is in us…

Let us GIVE THANKS for that
        consummation of all things
which the Spirit is working out in us ❖

THANK YOU!

The Call to Common Ground

This is a time of chaos.
This is a time for healing.
This is a time of choice.
This is a time to care.
This is a time to stand and say "yes."
This is a time to stand and say "no."
This is a time of challenge.
This is a time for peace.

We join together—
    old and young
        frail and strong
            hearts and hands
to heal the wounds
    we have wrought for centuries.

There is blood in our waters,
    acid in our land,
        death in our skies.

We join together to take up
    the sword of truth
        and the shield of light
to dissolve all boundaries,
    deceit, and judgment,

to stand united once again—I and thou
    in the garden of brotherhood.
The human heart is common ground.

From Common Ground, 1991, by Sarah Riely, Publisher, Connecting Arizona, Phoenix, Arizona

This ritual is ONE❖
The food is ONE❖
We who offer the food are ONE❖
The fire of hunger is also ONE❖
All action is ONE❖
We who understand this are ONE❖

An ancient Hindu blessing
before meals ∞∞∞—

We are what we think ❖

All that we are arises with our thoughts ❖

With our thoughts we make the world ❖

Speak or act with an impure mind

And trouble will follow you

As the wheel follows the ox that draws the cart ❖

Speak or act with a pure mind

And happiness will follow you

As your shadow, unshakable ❖

from *The Dhammapada: The Sayings of the Buddha,*
rendered into English by Thomas Byrom ❖

We cannot Love God unless we love each other, and to love each other we must know each other in the breaking of bread and we are not alone any more ❖ ❖ ❖ Heaven is a banquet and life is a banquet, too, even with a crust, where there is companionship ❖ LOVE

❖ comes

 Dorothy Day

❖ with

❖ community.

We come to join in

the banquet of love ❖

Let it open our hearts

and break down the fears

that keep us from

loving each other ❖

Sung by Dominican nuns
on special occasions at mealtime

We thank Thee for our daily bread

Let, also, Lord, our souls be fed

O, Bread of Life, from day to day

Sustain us on our homeward way ✣

Amen ✤

The Eckhardt family

The Peace of Wild Things

When despair for the world grows in me
and I wake in the night at the least sound
in fear of what my life and
my children's lives may be,
I go and lie down where the wood drake
rests in his beauty on the water,
and the great heron feeds.
I come into the peace of wild things
who do not tax their lives with forethought
of grief. I come into the presence of still water.
And I feel above me the day-blind stars
waiting with their light. For a time
I rest in the grace of the world,
and am free.

Wendell Berry

Where two or three are gathered
together in Thy name,
Thou hast promised to be in their midst.
Grant that we may be channels
for Thy love in the world
And awaken our souls to the
knowledge of Thy healing powers.

And may the peace of joy be with you.

Indralaya, Eastsound, Washington

This prayer is used to send healing thoughts.
Visualize the person who needs to be healed
and speak the name of that person aloud
before saying the final line of the prayer.

Marcia and **Jack Kelly** are writers who live in New York City. They are working on a series of books called *Sanctuaries: A Guide to Lodgings in Monasteries, Abbeys, and Retreats of the United States*, the first of which is already published. Their research has so far taken them to more than two hundred monasteries, and many of the graces in this book were collected on these travels ◈

Christopher Gausby is an artist who makes illuminated manuscript books of his own writings, combining the language and forms of modern art and philosophy with those of traditional art and spirituality. He also produces works of calligraphy on commission. He lives in New York City ◈